Magical Moments of
Living a Multidimensi[onal]

Divine Destiny Publishing

Suzanna Magic

Connect with Suzanna
www.suzannahealer.co.uk
colourfulsuz@gmail.com
fb.me/suzannasunflowersanctuary

Copyright © 2023 by Divine Destiny Publishing and Mary Gooden

All Rights Reserved. Apart from any fair dealing for the purposes of research or private study, or criticism or review, as permitted under the Copyright, Designs and Patents Act 1988, this publication may only be reproduced, stored or transmitted, in any form or by any means, with the prior permission in writing of the copyright owner, or in the case of the reprographic reproduction in accordance with the terms of licensees issued by the Copyright Licensing Agency. Enquiries concerning reproduction outside those terms should be sent to the publisher.

Contents

Gratitude Poem
INTRODUCTION TO MRS MAGIC.......1
Me, Myself, and I Poem
The name - Mrs Magic
SOUL JOURNEY TO A NEW ME AND THE BIRTH OF 'MAGICAL' MOMENTS OF A MYSTIC.......7
Deep Inside
Cracked open - a new beginning
Rebirth
Emerging as Mrs. Suzanna Magic
Too many times - past life memories
New Shoes
Calling
The gift in a dream
The call of LOVE
PAST LIFE MEMORIES AND ANCIENT WISDOM.......21
Suzanna - the story of my adopted first name. Part 1
Suzanna
Crystal Healing in Atlantis
High Priestess of COLOUR
Temple Dancers In Ancient Egypt
Queen Hathor
Flying with Lizzi
Persecution of a Gentle Maiden
Trial or Accusation?
Dread!
The Crystal Skull
The power of the patriarchy

Stabbed!
A Maiden with Healing gifts
Etruscan Women's Group
Old Acquaintance
Initiation in the Temple of the Rose
Seed Mother
Called to a crop circle
HEALING.......67
Something about me
Angelic Presence
The Dark Prince
Lost child
A gift of a Dragon
Fear of Gestapo
Letting go
Ana
Soul journeying
Preparation for birth
Working with fertility
Close Encounters with the Medical Profession and
Aiding healing with visualisation and crystals
VISIONS and DREAMS.......95
Chakra Flow
Reforming chemical bonds
The Coachman
The Gold shoes
Opening - a vision
New Purple Wings
Pink Tara's Gift
Lady's smock
Transformation with Archangels

Sister Moon
So spoke the Ash
EARTH HEALING GRIDS and PORTALS.......110
Setting Energy Grids around the World
A Thousand Petalled Lotus
A Visit to Stonehenge
The Merry Maidens Standing Stones in Cornwall
Arbor Low
Connecting the Rings
Nine Ladies
Visiting Glastonbury and Avebury
Labyrinth walk
Ely Cathedral
Golden Caribbean Grid
Puerto Vallarta Mexico 1
Opening a Portal at Puerto Vallarta 2
LYON
Finale Poem - Gifts
About the Author.......137
Reader Love.......140

GRATITUDE POEM TO ALL THOSE
WHO ENCOURAGED ME

<u>I've crossed a bridge!</u>

After listening to Whitney Houston
Singing
'Step by step'
I heard the line
'There's a bridge and a river
That I still must cross'

In my vision I saw
A verrry looooong suspension bridge
Spanning a wide river
I thought I had a very long
Journey ahead of me
Not sure I could make it alone!
Then I realised I was almost across
Only 1/8th of the bridge
To cross.

All that was behind me was
GRAY
The path in front of me was
BRIGHT
Leading to the
LIGHT
I only had a short way to go
To
JOY.

Suddenly I came to a place
Where I was
STUCK
Standing on
A line I could not cross
Alone
Bewildered
Bereft

One by one
You all arrived
Lined up beside me
A row of
Wonderful Women
Right across the bridge
Standing beside me.
Standing with me

A huge dark storm appeared
Thunder clashed
Lightning flashed
Wild winds blew
Black clouds raced overhead
Trying to push me back
With force
I was afraid
Turned around to run

You all stayed calm
Stood strong beside me
Faced the storm with me
Kept me safe
Kept me on the line
One wise woman stepped forward
Encouraged me on

Another pushed me lightly
From behind
Giving me a
'Helping hand'

I fell forward
Through the storm
Discovered I had wings
To carry me further
On my journey
I spread my wings
and
FLEW !!!!

I'm so proud to say
I have made it across that bridge
Arrived in a new land of
BRIGHTNESS
HOPE
JOY
RECOGNITION

Looking back
I can see you all
Clapping
Cheering
Celebrating with me
MY
SUCCESS

A golden wise woman
Approaches me
With a huge smile
Hands me a crystal chalice
Full of the elixir of life
My prize for showing
RESILIANCE
PERSISTENCE
FAITH

She invites me to
Take a sip
Of the nectar
Enter a new world
A new life
A new era!
AMEN

I'D LIKE TO THANK YOU
EACH AND EVERY ONE OF YOU
AMAZING WOMEN
FOR STANDING WITH ME
KEEPING ME SAFE
CHAMPIONING ME
I'M SO HONOURED TO HAVE YOU ALL
IN MY LIFE

WITH MUCH HEART FELT LOVE
SUZANNA MAGIC
X

INTRODUCTION TO MRS. MAGIC

Me, Myself and I

I am Suzanna Magic
I am a mother, grandmother
friend, homemaker,
mentor,
teacher, healer,
soul guide.

I have Spiritual gifts
Psychic powers
Magical empathy
I can tap into another's essence
Celebrate
And
Encourage them.

I welcome souls
Nurture and Guide them
On their journey
Here on Earth
and
In other realms.

I soar
Through the universe
Visiting stars and planets
Gathering wisdom
Bringing understanding.

I channel light to others
and to our beautiful planet Earth
Promoting personal and
Planetary healing.

I have dreams
And visions of times gone by
Access to
Many dimensions
Ancient wisdoms
Karmic patterns
Akashic records
I set energy grids across the planet
Connecting sacred sites
Opening portals of healing
Creating golden webs.

I work with Goddess energies
Crystals, colour
Helping the Divine Feminine
Return to Earth.

I LOVE and embrace being ME
I honour my gifts
And wish to share them
With many, many people
All over the world
And throughout
The Universe
To bring
LOVE
PEACE
HARMONY
FELLOWSHIP
COOPERATION
xx

The name - Mrs. Magic

I've been 'called'
To help many children
'Labelled' for not fitting in
I've worked across all age ranges and abilities
In many different educational settings

In one school
I was assigned 60 'labelled' children
Deemed to need extra help.
Handed some homemade games in a
Broken plastic basket
Given a large bean bag
Upon which we could sit
Shown a place in a cloakroom
Where we could work.
These I handed back
As they were beneath the dignity
Of the children and myself.
I agreed to accept the job
Providing I could work in a class room
Worthy of the children
And my expertise!

With reluctance I was offered the Art room
Which turned out to be a true 'God send'
I transformed this room
Into a special needs unit
Utilizing the art materials
For the children to
Express themselves
Displayed their work for all to see
I provided my own resources

Games, books, puzzles,
Created a library corner
Allowed the children to explore
Their own interests.
And create freely.

On entering my room one day
The headteacher looked around amazed
She asked
'Who has done all this work?'
'The children' I replied
'They illustrate the stories we read
Research their own projects
Make models, paint, draw
Bake
Write poetry
Concoct recipes'
'I can hardly believe these children
Could have done all this'
Responded the headteacher.

The educational psychologist
Came to visit the school
'I had to come and meet you
To see for myself what you do.
We call you MRS MAGIC
As you transform these children
But we have no idea how!!'

It was not really magic!
I treated the children like people
Accepted them as the unique individuals they are
Let them follow their interests
Express who they are
I didn't try to fix them
Or
Make them
Fit in.

The Truth is I saw
BEYOND THE LABELS

Nurtured these children
Helped them discover their
Own gifts
Connect to their souls
Explore their calling.

I like the 'label'
MRS. MAGIC
So I have adopted it as my name!!!
I've been on a long journey of
Honing my spiritual gifts
Teaching
Counselling
Healing
Integrating my wisdom,
Intuition and expertise
Now I stand in my truth
Accept my power
As
MRS SUZANNA MAGIC !!!

SOUL JOURNEY TO A NEW ME
AND
THE BIRTH OF 'MAGICAL MOMENTS OF A MYSTIC'

Deep Inside

In my morning reverie
I fell
Deep inside
my soul

First I found a
Book
An ancient book full of
Poetry
Wise words
Healing balms

Next I saw a
Box-
The lid slowly rose up
And a
HUGE RED HEART
Floated out
followed by
a never ending stream
of
red hearts.

I am ready
To release these
Wise, magical words
And expand my
LOVE
Into the world
Bringing
DEEP HEALING
TRANSFORMATION
UNDERSTANDING
PEACE.

Cracked open – a new beginning

As I awoke in my warm bed
Very early this morning
Stirring from a Full moon dream
I felt my outer- shell
Like a plaster statue
Cracking down the middle
From head to toe
Falling away in two halves
Releasing a dazzling bright light
Which shone forth
Flying free
Revealing my true essence brilliance
A resurrection
I have reached another level
Of consciousness.

Rebirth

Down
    Down
        Down
To a cold dark place
Devoid of love
No Light
    No Colour
        No Warmth
Curled like a foetus
Under the duvet
Shivering
Iced to the core
No joy in life
No point in existing
Deeper
    Deeper
        Deeper
Through fear
to
ABJECT TERROR
No will to breathe
My body hurts
My heart slows
Struggling to beat
WHY?
What happened??

I'm 'told'
Something so awful occurred
In a past life
I'm not allowed to know
I have
So many tears to release

After days of sleep
Nurturing with warmth
Self-love
I s l o w l y pulled through
TO BE REBORN
I've passed through a dark night of the soul
Another abyss crossed
I'm
Cleansed
Lighter
Brighter
TRANSFORMED
I'm back on my soul's path
Of universal truth
And
Understanding

Emerging as Mrs. Suzanna Magic

I have walked my path
Gone wherever I was called
Worked from my heart
Touched many souls
Changed many lives
Taken light into places of darkness
With little or no support!!
I have experienced
Ridicule
Putdown
Challenge
But I have carried on.

Many saw the effects of my work
But could not attribute it to me
Who I am
My softness, gentleness, acceptance
Or understand how I achieved
such remarkable results.

I'm left feeling vulnerable
Invisible
Mis-understood
Exhausted
Isolated

Now I am entering my
Age of Wisdom
The Wise woman
Phase of my life
I wish to present myself
In a different way
Share my
Knowledge, wisdom, experience
PRESENCE

WHO AM I ?
I AM A SOUL GUIDE
SPIRITUAL TEACHER
HEALER
SEER
MEDIUM
CHANNELLER OF DIVINE FEMININE ENERGY
GRID SETTER
EARTH HEALER
MYSTIC
I wish to expand my visibility
Have a greater impact
To bring the world into a
New Age

Too many times - past life memories

Why do I hang my head
And hide
When all I wish to do is
SHINE
Love, Heal
Nurture
Offer a helping hand
To others
Along their path

Too many times
In past lives
I have been
Vilified, Ridiculed
Beaten, Tortured,
Accused, Shackled,
Hung, Silenced
For my mystical gifts.

I have returned
To right the wrongs
Cleanse, heal my wounds
Bring light, understanding
Welcome other mystical souls
To Earth
Guide them on their adventure of
Seeing
Hearing
Sensing
Healing
Magic

Working with other realms
Elementals, Devas
Angels, Goddesses
and Wise Beings
To bring Harmony
Peace and LOVE
To Earth

New Shoes

I had a dream one night
I was lost and had wondered into
A large building full of books and
Shoes!
Boxes piled high.
I sat and rested - looked down at my shoes -
Clear jelly wedges
Comfortable, shabby, worn out, broken
'Invisible shoes!'

I needed NEW SHOES
More of the same perhaps?
But NO
The angelic helper refused to give me those
She brought me large gold clogs-
Much too heavy for me,
High heeled shoes- glamorous -
But far too high
And uncomfortable.

I looked around and searched
I noticed others looking too
Some seemed to know what they wanted
Left quickly with head held high.
Others hid in the shadow
Hoping never to be seen
Cowering away from life.

Eventually I found my type of shoe-
But there was only one!
A beautiful sandal -a jelly shoe again
Very, very comfortable, flexible and soft
Transparent in the middle
With GOLD pointed toes, Gold kitten heals
Elegant, cute, light
A perfect fit for me

BUT
Where was the other one?
Another search began
Soul search, deep longing to find the other shoe
Eventually the helper found it
I had my pair of new shoes!

Elated, daring
I put on my new shoes
Embellished in gold, elegant
Comfortable
NEW
I could easily move in these
Shine a little more
I felt uplifted, took off my old coat too
Left it on the chair.
I exited the building of lessons
Light, bright ready
To 'fly' along my new path
In my new world

Calling

A golden light
Shone
Behind my eyes

I glowed
Tingled
Scintillated
Shone

My body
Realigned
Preparing me to
Step forward
In
My role
As
MATRIARCH
DIVINE GODDESS
CONNECTED

Bringing
TRUTH
UNDERSTANDING
CLARITY
HEALING
TRANSFORMATION
GUIDANCE

I am ready
To step forward
With
LOVE

The gift in a dream

I'd had a difficult week
Soul journeying
Through darkness
Reaching deep depths of
Despair
Fear
Abandonment.
Then one night
I had this dream
I was sitting up in bed
Dressed in a pure white robe
A white box was handed to me
Down from the heavens
I removed the lid
Unwrapped white tissue paper
Within I found a copy
Of MY book !!
With shiny Magenta cover
And gold script announcing
'Magical Moments of a Mystic'
By
Suzanna Magic
And I heard a voice say
'This will be a gift to the universe'

I smiled
Felt blessed
Light!
What a wonderful gift
Of a dream

The call of LOVE

Answering the call of LOVE
The inner voice to
Growth, fulfilment
Soul opportunity
I choose to be more visible
More accessible
Share my experiences, knowledge
Wisdom with many
In the name of LOVE
And TRUTH
Stand up and be counted
Spread the light
WRITE
PUBLISH
SPEAK
Be heard, be seen
Guide others on their soul path
I have chosen the call of
LOVE
x

PAST LIFE MEMORIES
AND
ANCIENT WISDOM

I can soar through the universe
Visiting stars
Planets
Moons
Galaxies
Gathering wisdom
Bringing understanding.

Suzanna- the story of my adopted first name.
Part 1

Suzanna is not my given name but one I resonate with. When I first had flashbacks to this past life of my soul, Suzanna was a courtesan leading a 'privileged' but very restricted and unfulfilling life in the court of Louis 16th in France, residing in the Palais du Louvre, Paris.
Suzanna was not allowed out of the court and certainly not allowed to voice her concerns about people starving and in need of care or in any way communicate with or help the proletariat even though her heart craved to do so. Suzanna was aware of great inequality in life; the plight of the starving, ailing masses and was determined to help.

At night Suzanna would don old clothes and a hooded cape and sneak out of the palace under cover of darkness to administer food, medicinal herbs and remedies, tend to the poor and needy, sneaking back into the palace before dawn to put on her fine clothes and resume her 'privileged', sad life.
I recognised my soul name and my essence quality of helping the needy realising this soul part of me has returned to continue Suzanna's mission in this present incarnation.
I adopted my full 'spiritual' name of Suzanna as my professional name on first remembering the life of Suzanna, courtesan to King Louis 16th and have used it since.

****

Part 2
A LATER INSIGHT-continuation of Suzanna's plight.
On a more recent trip to Paris I was experiencing sharp pains running across my lower back and wondered 'Why?'

I had further insights and flashbacks to the life of Suzanna, Louis' courtesan, as I was nearing the Palais de Louvre, Louis' palace and my home many many years ago. I found myself walking through the Tuileries garden in a kind of trance with dark and fearful thoughts invading my mind and pains cursed through my body. My neck hurt, my legs hurt and oh the pulsating pain in my back!!

Through dreams and energy work I have been able to release these pains and understand their origin.

Suzanna 'remembered' and envisioned being betrayed by other courtesans as she returned from one of her secret outings to help the poor and needy. Two men in particular betrayed Suzanna, one a very vindictive older man and one young rather innocent man who was easily influenced by the older man.

The older man accused Suzanna of being a traitor and stealing from the king's pantry. He disliked her intensely and was determined to stop her from helping the poor.

Suzanna was beaten, shackled, imprisoned, tried and condemned to death! On being led out to be hanged Suzanna stood tall proclaiming

'I am not guilty of theft. I have been doing what was morally just- tending to and feeding the poor, sick and needy'

Suzanna had a great desire to scream out-

'When will they ever learn?'

-but stifled this scream, remained silent, held her head high and prepared for her fate of hanging.

No wonder I was in pain as this deep trauma was released from my body.

*****

This 'scream' has been trapped in my energetic body and was released in this life during a healing session.
I 'saw' Suzanna's spirit body departing, glad to escape from such unjust times but the release was bitter sweet.
Letting go of all this trapped past life trauma from my body has been quite a painful process. I had been feeling a deep irrational fear of speaking up at this point in my life- now I understand why.

****

In my present incarnation I have helped many people - especially misunderstood children, poor families and sensitives.
My soul is an essence of 'Suzanna' returned to continue her mission.
From very early childhood I'd always had an inner 'knowing' that my correct name was Suzanna .
To me, the name Suzanna feels whole, complete, fulfilling, meaningful and energizing.
It is now my adopted name.

Suzanna

Suzanna-
18th century me
Courtesan in the inner sanctum
Of King Louis 16th
Of France
Society divided
Poverty rife
Inégalité normale
Bounded by tradition
My heart full of warmth
But heavy sadness
At night
I donned a hooded cape
Old clothes
Snook out of the palace
Under cover of darkness
Carrying baskets of food
Herbs, remedies
To help the poor
Returning just before dawn
To dress in finery
Resume my unfulfilling
Life of privilege.

One dawn as I returned
Entered an ill-lit secret passage
Running under the Palace
Hood over my head
Carrying now empty baskets

Behold-
In front of me stood
Two men
'STOP!' they commanded
'Where have you been?'
I removed my hood
Showed my face
Stood straight to face them
'I've been distributing food
Remedies to the poor'
I answered proudly
'So - stealing from the Palace stores-
TRAITOR to the king!'
'Arrest this girl!!'
'I've been doing what is morally just' I defied.

They dragged me by my arms
Led me to the court
Betrayed my exploits
To help the poor
I was found guilty
Imprisonment
Held hostage
Condemned to death.

Led out to be hanged
I stood tall and proud
Announced
'I am no traitor
I was doing what is morally just
Ministering to the poor'
Noose placed around my neck
I faced my plight with dignity
Stifling a wish to scream
'When will they understand?'.

My spirit departed
Left my body
Bitter sweet release
Glad to fly away
From this heartless life of
Privileged
Injustice

I am Suzanna
My soul now returned
Continuing my mission
Taking light
Into dark places
Helping the
Poor
Needy
Neglected
Forgotten
Misunderstood
Abandoned
Spreading
Divine feminine gifts
Of
ACCEPTANCE
JUSTICE
SHARING
HARMONY
NURTURE
LOVE

Crystal Healing in Atlantis

I travelled back in time
Found myself
In the ancient realm
Of Atlantis
A very advanced civilisation
Of divine wisdom
Conscious understanding

In this incarnation
I was a young maiden
A crystal healer
Working in the temple
Alongside the priestesses
Healing children
With crystals of different colours
And vibrations
Releasing trauma
From the children's bodies
Restoring them to
Well-being

I had a young lover
We were twin souls
Destined to spend our lives
Together
This young man
Was an innocent
Pure of soul
One day he asked me
To accompany him
To see the great crystal
And meet a group of people
Who had drawn him in

Warily
I followed him
Became suspicious
And felt ill at ease
Amongst these people
Who it transpired
Were trying to subvert
The magic of the crystal

During a healing session
In the temple
I saw myself kneeling by a child
Prone on a raised platform
I became aware of a huge commotion
People shouting, people running
Fleeing the temple
I stayed with the children
Tending them
Calming them

Water started to enter the temple
Slowly rising
News arrived
The folly of a few
Had caused an explosion
Of the great crystal of Atlantis
Creating a tsunami
Flooding the island
Eventually
Submerging it
Destroying everything
Bringing to an end
A wonderous civilisation

Some people escaped
Carrying knowledge and divine wisdom
With them
Establishing new civilisations
In Ancient Egypt
Ancient Greece
Based on Divine connection
Re-establishing Atlantean traditions

High Priestess of COLOUR

In a vision
I saw myself
Standing proud
Dressed in a long flowing robe
Adorned with a
Crescent Moon headdress

I was a High Priestess of COLOUR

I sat with the Higher Counsel
Bringing wisdom
Truth
Teaching others
Bringing understanding of vibration
Colour
Crystal

We used colour in the healing temples
Where rooms were set aside for
Energy Healing
The sun's rays poured in
Through windows of beautiful crystal.
Each colour had its own frequency
Each room was used for
Bathing in that vibration
Bringing shifts, healing
And comfort
On many levels

To choose just two examples
Amethyst brought CALMNESS
Nervous renewal
Higher understanding
Rose Quartz brought unconditional love
Nurture
Softness

We also used colour and crystals
In birthing pools
To alleviate pain
Ease the new souls passage
Into this world
Each pool was surrounded by crystals
Which the new mother
Was encouraged to use
By the wise women
Depending on their need.

These ancient wisdoms
Return to Earth today
Lie deep within my soul
And the souls of others returning
With this wisdom
I have helped many
To find ease in their lives
Using the vibration of
Colour and Crystal.

Temple Dancers In Ancient Egypt

Dancing in the temple
In Ancient Egypt
Me a temple dancer
He a young priest
Twin souls
Twirling lightly
Robes of white
Ethereal beauty
Floating freely
Trance achieved
Spirits risen
Holy voice
Message given
Levitation
Lifting of the souls
Freeing of the spirits
Bringing laughter
Mirth
Friends forever
Hereafter

Queen Hathor

Queen of Egypt
Wise of soul
Followed God
Understood Truth

Her son was tempted
Drawn away
His soul enticed
He walked away

Hathor followed
Out of love
She tried to save him
Bring him back

He had free choice
He turned away
Threw a dagger
Into her leg

Her heart cried out
For her lost son
His soul was lost
It paid the price

It now returns
To try again
We meet once more
I feel the love
I sense the pain
In my right leg

I understand
My heart cries out
I try to save your soul again
You are not convinced
You make your choice
You walk away

I did my best
To share the truth
To show the way
So you could stay
My heart is reft
I let you go

Flying with Lizzi

Flying
Way back in time
To Ancient Egypt
The temple of the pyramids.
Flying
A High priestess connecting
Heaven to earth
Within the inner sanctum,
A sacred place,
Protected, revered, safe
Conducting rituals
Of higher wisdom,
Channelling pure white light
From source
Cared for by a trusted friend
Goddess of sacred oils and balms
Caressed, anointed
Cherished
A treasured friendship
Of reverence, understanding
Deep soul love,
AWE
Revived and rekindled
In the here and now

With LOTS of LOVE and GRATITUDE
To Lizzi

A Past Life memory
Part 1

Persecution of a Gentle Maiden

She was sitting
on a mossy bank
Surrounded by wild flowers,
nature
Talking to a small audience
About herbs, healing
Sharing her wisdom.

A harsh sound
came rushing through
the woods
A marauding gang of
Men appeared
Wielding tools
Swords, spears.

They had heard of
Her magic
Special powers
Skills
Felt threatened by her
Female gifts
Her abilities
to see, hear
Communicate with
Other realms.

Following came the Overlords
Dressed in black
Mounted on horses
They encircled her
Separated her
Started questioning
her 'authority'
In their kingdom

"I've merely come in peace
and kindness" she said
"To heal, share knowledge
Care, teach.
I offer my skills
To any and all
Who wish to receive.
I am no threat
to you.
I do not want your land
Or wish to rule
I am a gentle soul
With gifts of healing
To offer."

"WITCH" she heard
Followed by
Shouting and unrest
"Don't trust her!"
Came the cry

Suddenly she felt
A searing pain
As a poisoned arrow
Entered the arch
On her left foot

'How sad,' she thought
'They are unwilling
and unable
to accept kindness,
divine love.'

The poison travelled
up her leg
Her heart began to pound
She became light headed
Faint
Felt as though
she was going to die.
The effects of
'Belladonna',
Deadly nightshade
she recognised!

A lordsman
Seized her
Hoisted her
Onto his horse
Whisked her away

The young maiden
Did survive
Fought off the poison
Her soul spared
So she could continue
Her work.

They questioned her
Tried to understand
But did not have
Her skills.
They beat her
Starved her
Raped her
Until a young lord
Asked her
To teach him

Her heart fluttered
At his kindness
She stayed,
Worked with him
Developed healing balm
To help
His people
Created an apothecary,
Trained administrators.

He thanked her,
Offered her a reward
"What would you like?"
He asked
"My freedom" she replied
"and
Guaranteed protection
So I may
Spread my
Work to heal
Others"

"It's yours," he said
"I also give you a home
To return to
Whenever you wish
and
My heart
is always yours."

Part 2.

<u>Trial or Accusation?</u>

I saw myself
In mediaeval times.
As a young maiden
Dressed in a long
Green robe
Tied at the waist with a cord
Hair shining brightly.

Yank-I felt a pain in my arm
As I was pulled
By guards
Grasping me tightly
Dragging me
Into a courtroom

The room was packed
With gray people
I was taken to face a large table
Where many men were sitting
Fear rose within
Overwhelming me.

I stood still
Breathed deeply
Regained my countenance
Caught the eye
Of one young lord
Felt myself
Become poised once more

'This young woman
Stands accused
Of seeking power
Claiming to be a
Healer using herbs
And magic'
Boomed a deep voice
Over the heckling crowd.
'What will become of her?'

The young Lord stood
Agreed to take me
In his charge
Keep me safe
Relief flooded through me
I was escorted away
To join his people

The young lord
Showed patience, gentleness
In time
Persuaded me
To talk to him
About my healing gifts

His kindness
Opened my heart
I began to trust him
And teach him
My ways

I stayed in his charge
Agreed to work for him
Sharing my healing skills
With others
For the benefit of all

Finally I regained
My freedom
Lifelong protection
To continue
My healing work.

Dread!

I awoke with aching pains
In both knees
What now? I wondered
What can this be??

As I drifted back into slumber
Asking for release
A scenario unfolded
Where I was with two old friends
In a witches' house
On the edge of the woods
Remembered from times
Gone by

'Can anybody survive this?'
I was asking
'I'll tell you how' replied one friend
As she began to read from a 'story' book
To our other friend
Whilst offering her a drink.

I felt fear, anxiety arise
Unsure of what was unfolding
I turned towards the door
To leave and
Could see white poison added to the drink
To end a life.

Dread, deep fear left my knees
As she nodded to me and said
'This was the only way
There were instructions
I had to follow
So we two could survive
To carry on our work'.

I startled awake
In a state of shock
Felt dull, nauseous
Overwhelmed
Wondered
How much more of this
Clearing could I take??
*
But I am glad my knees have been released.

The Crystal Skull

Visiting the museum of mankind
In London
I was drawn to look at
A crystal skull
Of Mayan origin
Quite fascinating!!

As I approached the skull
I felt my mind and soul
Connect with it
'Share what you know'
Said the skull
'You have wisdom to bring
To the world'
My third eye opened
Connected with the crystal
I instantly understood how
These skulls were made
an apparent mystery to others!

The power of the patriarchy

I had accepted the very kind invitation of a dear friend to dine as guests at her husband's college.

The college was a very old well established college at a prestigious university. After we had assembled and been greeted in an ancient reception room, we entered the main dining hall and were shown to our seats. The dining hall was grand but quite dark, fusty and cold. It was lit by candles as it would have been in ancient times but had an austere, unwelcoming atmosphere. I felt quite ill at ease and out of place in this setting.

Part way through the dinner I felt a chill pass over me. My eyes were drawn upwards and I noticed that all the way around the room hung a gallery of portraits of elderly men, former dons of the college, all of whom seem to be looking straight at me.

Suddenly without warning a dark swirl of energy swept around the room connecting all the pictures and bolting like a dart into my heart. I felt stabbed, wounded, deeply hurt, violated, vulnerable.

I became quite faint, felt very cold, shocked, attacked and trapped.

The portraits' eyes stared down on me.

I'd witnessed the collective energy of the patriarchy trying to eliminate my female soul light.

I just wished for the meal to end so I could bid a hasty farewell and return home to recover my equilibrium, escape the dons.

The power of the patriarchy had struck again.

But- who would believe me - a young female guest in this realm of patriarchy???

Stabbed!!

Seated in the ancient dining hall
Lit by candlelight
I felt uncomfortable
In such an austere atmosphere

Suddenly a chill crept through me
I looked up and noticed
A gallery of portraits
Hung all around the room
Portraits of elderly gentleman
All former dons
In this ancient college

As I watched
I was aware of a dark energy
Swirling around the room
Building together
Joining the portraits
When suddenly
It darted towards me
Bolting into my heart

I felt stabbed
Attacked
Demeaned
Violated
Vulnerable
All the portraits' eyes
Were upon me
Their patriarchal energy
Trying to quench
My Divine feminine soul.

A Maiden with Healing gifts

Arriving to stay
In a holiday cottage
On a country estate
I immediately felt
'At home'
Certain I had lived there before
During my stay
This feeling was
Reinforced as
I seemed to travel
Back and forth
Between times
Touching aspects
Of my past life and my present

I felt a huge affinity
With the Manor and its history
A comfortable warm relationship
I became aware
I was not of the Manor
But a young maiden
Living on the estate
Favoured by the Lord
Cherished as a beloved daughter
These feelings persisted
During a delightful few days

On my return home
A reverie fell upon me
I saw myself once again
As the young maiden
Wearing pink robes
Hooded cape
Carrying a basket of herbs
And remedies.
I tended the sick and needy
In the village
Spent many hours
At the Manor house
Welcomed honoured
Respected revered
Was fondly championed
Supported in my craft
I felt protected and safe
Free to be me

As this young healing maiden
I was of a charmed nature
Quiet
Gentle
Loving
Kind
Soft
Gifted in the healing arts
Cherished for these traits
Looked after
Cared for
Accepted
Encouraged
And loved gently in return

Never-the-less
The young maiden felt alone
Had a yearning
To return 'home'
Away from the sorrows
And pains on earth
One eve she lay down
Passed over peacefully
In her sleep
Her soul
Becoming a rainbow angel
Assisting for eternity
From heaven

Etruscan Women's Group

I went on a dance holiday to Turkey with 8 women friends. The leader of our group asked if I would lead a meditation for the group one evening. I walked into the local town wanting to find something appropriate to wear. The owner of the shop went into the back and came out with a lovely blue dress appliqued with traditional Turkish crochet saying 'This was just right for you'.

I tried it, agreed I liked it, took it back to our villa and then noticed the dress had the label DIANA in it! Of course it was right for me! I often channelled Diana, a moon goddess. Then I realised that it was a full moon that night too!

We walked up the steps of the Kursk- a raised covered platform with open sides-where large cushions were arranged in a circle ready for the meditation. With some trepidation I set out my coloured silks and we began the meditation journey- I was not even sure who would join in and follow me! Everyone opened up, enjoyed the meditation and responded to the message I gave them that we had sat in circles together in a previous life and had been called back together now.

The following day one of the ladies asked me if I could find out more about our previous connection.

I went into a deep meditation and was given a vision of the Etruscan times with each of us playing a major part in that society.

We were drawn together again to re-touch our inner strength and qualities from Etruscan times, bringing ancient ideals and wisdom forward for self-recognition, mutual support and renewed strength to foster these qualities in society today.

The Etruscan women worked together cooperatively to run society and were supportive of each other's roles and needs. Everyone used their natural talents and abilities for the higher good to create a harmonious and peaceful society and to fulfil their soul purpose.
Women and men were equal in society, each understood and respected their roles.
This is the vision I had and the roles played by us in Etruria.

AT THE TEMPLE OF VENUS - dedicated to the female arts.
I was the high priestess, with a pure essence communing with higher realms to bring spiritual wisdom, healing, blessing and understanding

One lady was a young priestess and trance temple dancer. She was very sensitive, very gentle and of a delicate nature.

Another was a priestess and temple dancer with responsibility for welcoming others to the temple. She had a very gentle, dignified energy.

One lady was a herbalist making healing remedies from plants and flowers using sacred knowledge. She was wise, non - judgemental and skilled.
In present day she is an aromatherapist.

Our trip coordinator was an alter dresser, bringing natural gifts to temple alter for ceremonies and blessings. She was always exuberant, happy and singing, a friend to all and a free spirit.

One lady was a scribe - interpreting, writing and delivering spiritual truths from the temple to the village - a go between role requiring great inner strength.

One lady was a sage-femme (wise woman)-keeping an eye on souls' wellbeing, fostering higher understanding and soul healing. Also bringing new souls to the temple for their blessing ceremony. She was very wise, strong, determined. In present life she was a midwife- une sage-femme!

One lady was a village elder responsible for making laws, especially concerned with women's welfare and status. She had leadership qualities, was practical, strong and well respected.

One lady was the head of the 'mothers union' overseeing, advising and teaching women's roles, sorting out disputes, keeping peace and harmony.
She was very practical, compassionate and strong.

All of us have incarnated into this current life with these same qualities and skills they had in Etruscan times. Each of us is strong, wise and resilient and have brought our deep inner knowing, our own gifts to help nurture others and create harmony today.

Old Acquaintance

As I sat weaving my basket
A new student joined the class
Sat next to me
Engaged in conversation
Asked about my healing

Several days later
She came to me
For healing and a chat
Said she was drawn to be with me
Felt we should meet

This new acquaintance invited me
To walk with her
In a local wood where she had felt
A strange sensation

As we walked
I felt fear, apprehension cursing through my veins
We stopped by a large tree
Where she was sure someone had been hanged

As I approached in trepidation
I 'saw' a corpse
Hanging from the tree
'It's me' I said
'In a past-life
We were enemies
You hanged me there'

'I'm so sorry she said
I knew I had to bring you here
To clear the air.'

We moved on
Karma complete
Went our separate ways.

Initiation in the Temple of the Rose

Invited into the Temple
Of the Rose
I entered
Welcomed by Goddess Kali
Who dressed me in
A beautiful magenta and gold sari
Seated me on a golden throne
Surrounded by delicate pink roses
Placed a glittering crown
Bejewelled with diamonds
And a rose pink Gem
Upon my head

Isis, Matriarch of the Moon
Descended
Wrapped her wings around me
For strength, protection
Courage
I saw Pachamama
Goddess of mother earth
Swathed in a cloak
Of eagle feathers
Sitting on the ground-
Despondent
Sad about the plight of our planet

Friends and kindred spirits
Congregated around me
One guarded the door
With a dragon!
One brought gentle pink light
For LOVE
One bathed my feet with oil
To soothe
One gave me rose elixir to sip
To nourish
One wrapped me in a green cloak
For balance
One gave me a pure white rose
With a golden centre
To cleanse

Kali anointed me
With rose perfumed essence
I was purified
I have reached another level
Of consciousness
My purpose clarified
I am a link between
Isis and Pachamama
Moon and Earth
I am here to channel
Divine feminine light
To the Planet
And all of life
Here on Earth
Be ready
to receive!!

Seed Mother

Long long ago
In the time of Lemuria
Everything was dark,
Gray
Without enough light

I was a young woman
Carer of children
Pure of heart and soul

One day there came
A bright light
From the sky -
A spaceship landed

A huge Lord,
A Light Being
Tall, luminous, glowing
Stepped out

'You have been chosen
To come with us'
He said to me
As I gather the children
Behind me
Warily

'No sir I cannot come
I have these children
To care for
I am their guardian'
I replied

'Others can care for the children
You are to come with me
You have been chosen
For the pureness of your soul
The love in your heart
You are needed'

'No sir, I will not leave
These children
They are entrusted
To my care'

'We honour your commitment
But you have been beckoned
To come with us
On a very special mission'

Someone stepped forward
From the shadows of a crowd
And said
'We will care for the children
You are being called
You must go
Where you are needed'

Hesitantly I stepped forward
The Light Being held out his hand
Helped me aboard the spaceship.

We travelled far far away
To a constellation called
The Pleiades
Where I stayed for a while
To learn their ways

I returned to earth
A SEED MOTHER
Impregnated to give birth
To a new generation
Who would bring
A higher light
To our Planet
Renewing the contract
Of soul journeying
To our Earth

Called to a crop circle

Restless
Unable to sleep
Called
Called

I rose very early
Paced the house
Unable to settle
Disturbed
Called
Called

I drove at the crack of dawn
To a nearby hill
Called
Called

I climbed
To the top of the hill
Called
Called
Feeling jittery yet
Following the call

I looked down
Into the field below
I saw magnificence-
A beautiful crop circle
Was in view
The atmosphere was charged
Mysterious

The circle had not been there
The day before
It appeared from nowhere
Calling my soul
Drawing me near

I stood mesmerised
For several minutes
As the sun rose
True magnificence
Was revealed
As I neared
The crop circle
I felt
Awe
Fear
Overwhelm
Alone
Wondered
Was I safe?
Vowed return
Take a closer look
In daylight

The following day
Out of the blue
Two healer friends
Contacted me
Asking if they could visit
We went together
To experience the circle
It was stunning
Perfectly formed
Each stem of wheat
Precisely bent

Into an intricate pattern
Culminating in a swirl
In the middle

As we approach the centre
The clouds parted
The sun beamed down upon us
Like a spot light
I felt guided
To give one friend
A deep healing
She received with gratitude
Strangely not many people
In my village
Were even aware
Of the circle's presence

I visited several times
Intrigued by the beauty
Of the patterns made
I felt privileged
Chosen
Called
To such a spectacular
Supernatural site
Of awe and wonder

HEALING

I channel light to others
and to the Earth
Releasing trauma
Promoting personal
and
Planetary healing.

Something about me

There must be something about me
That others sense or see
For I am often approached by strangers
Who start to tell me their life stories
Ask for guidance
Seek wisdom and
Solace.

Let me tell you about just a few

A colleague of my husbands
Who I had never met before
Came to a party at our home
Within minutes he was standing by my side
As I finished off some cooking in the kitchen
Spent the next hour telling me in great detail
About the illness and subsequent
Passing of his late wife!
Then went off to join the other guests!

A friend's flat mate
On hearing my voice
Was convinced he needed
Healing from me
To help him recover
He had been unwell for 3 years
No diagnosis could be found
I found he was possessed
By a dark spirit
Which I removed.
After the healing
Doctors were able to diagnose
His organs were in stress

At a party
I was happily chatting to guests
Thankful no one had told me their troubles
I went outside for a breath of air
Suddenly a woman I did not know
Came running up the path
'There you are I've been looking for you'
She said
She poured out all her woes
Cried
Wailed
I
Listened
Comforted
Hugged her
Then off she went back
To join the party!

After a swimming class
One of the ladies approached me and asked
'Are you a medium?'
'I can be' I replied
'Why do you ask?'
'My sister wants to see a medium-
Can I bring her to you?'
'Of course' I replied
And she did!
Her sister's curiosity about
A difficult situation
Was resolved
She left with peace of mind
A lighter heart.

Sitting on a bus
The lady next to me started a conversation
She'd had a really rough time
With complex knee problems
Which she told me all about
This was her first journey out
After a yearlong recovery
She was very anxious
At the end of the journey
I helped her off the bus
Wished her well.
Went on my way

This is how my life is
There must be something about me
Which others sense-
I often wonder
What??

Angelic Presence

I called upon the angelic realms
When healing my friend.
I felt a magnificent presence descend
And was aware of a dazzling
Bright light

The angel stood beside me,
Wrapped his wings around the healing couch
Offering comfort, deep peace,
Purification, protection
And pure love

My friend relaxed, drifted off then stirred
Feeling refreshed
Uplifted
Lightened
She smiled a beatific smile
Of inner peace
And oneness

The Dark Prince

I phoned my friend
His flatmate answered
We had a chat
I left a message
Asking for my friend
To call me back

My friend returned my call
Said his flatmate had inquired
'Who is the woman I spoke to?
I feel I'd like to have healing from her.'
We arranged to meet
My client said he'd felt unwell
For several years
He'd lost a lot of weight
But the medics
Could find no cause

I started the healing
Cleared away a lot of
Dense energy
Around him
SUDDENLY
A Dark Knight appeared !
Cloaked in heavy black
Head covered in a dark helmet
Plumed with the black feather
'Who are you?' I asked
'I'm the Dark Prince' he replied

Automatically
Very bright light emanated
From my heart
My soul
My hands
I focused with great determination
Willing the Dark Knight to leave
Eventually his darkness cracked open
The Dark Knight fell away
But not before
Grabbing me around the throat

I was rather undeserved
By this experience
Understood I had been sent a test
I went home with a croaky voice
And that night I did not sleep well
My mother and sister
Entered my dreams
'Take care and always ask
Who's there?
Before you start healing'
Came their advice

Next day I went to see my spiritual teacher
She removed vestiges of
The Dark Knight's energy
From my aura
Gave me a ritual to perform
With candles
Sound and crystals
To fully cleanse the healing room I'd used.

A few days later
My client phoned
He'd been in hospital having diagnostic tests
The doctors found
His organs were stressed
He thanked me for removing the Dark Prince
Said he'd known he was possessed
Felt as though he was being chased
For the last three years
He hadn't known who to seek help from
Until he heard my voice
Was eternally grateful for my help
He began to gain weight and recover
No longer felt fearful.
I'd been sent a very powerful challenge
My soul 'knew' what to do
I succeeded, I learned.

Lost child

Young woman
Expecting a child
Sat in front of me
At the healing centre
'I'm afraid'
She said
'I lost my first little girl
I'm so very
Very sad'

I had a vision of a young girl
Aged about 4
Standing beside her
'What did she look like'
I asked
She described the child I could see
Standing beside her

'Your daughter is here
Standing beside you
Smiling
She asked me to tell you
She is OK
Happy where she was now
Don't be sad anymore'

'THANK YOU THANK YOU'
The young mum cried
'I knew I had to come here today
I knew I had to see you
Now I can move on
Look forward to the birth
Of my new child'

The gift of a Dragon

The redhaired girl
Came for healing
She wanted to talk
Using crystals
To release old blocks

During the healing
She 'saw' me
Hand her a gift
Of a dark velvet bag

I asked her
Would you like to look inside?
On opening the bag
She took out a large egg
Which she held in her hands

I asked her
'Would you like to hatch the egg?'
She said she would
And as she held it to warm it
The egg cracked open

I asked her
'What was inside?'
She replied
'It's a small red dragon
Come to work with me'

I asked her
'Will you accept the Dragon?'
'Yes indeed!'
Was her response
The baby Dragon jumped onto
Her right shoulder

I asked
"Why have you got a baby Dragon?'
My client said
'I will nurture the Dragon
Learn to work with its fire energy'
She felt reunited
With an old knowledge
Of Dragon energy healing.

What a beautiful gift!

Fear of Gestapo

My client came to talk
Fear and anxiety
Had overtaken her
An acquaintance of hers
Had brought up a deep seated dread
To the surface
Causing her to flee and hide
Whenever this acquaintance appeared
She came to find out why

As we sat together
She began to shake
Could smell smoke
Feel a dark presence
Beside her
Causing her to panic
Who is it?
Why the fear?
She wanted to know.

We journeyed back together
To a tie gone by
In war torn France
I saw my client then as
A young man
Standing by a burning hay stack
Wrecked farm buildings
A Gestapo car parked nearby

Suddenly my client
Gasped
Touched her throat
'I can't breathe-
Help me
Such pain in my throat
Such fear!'

I 'saw' a Gestapo officer standing by her
With dark gloved hands
Which he placed around her throat
Gently squeezing

I used my vision
To guide the healing process
I asked her if she
Knew what was happening
'I'm being choked by this acquaintance
She was a man in those times'

I asked if she felt
Ready to find forgiveness and
Release the past
In tears she cried
' YES -I forgive
Let it go
Let it go'

The deep trauma trapped in her body
From eons ago
Had been released
She returned to being
Her present self
Glad she had understanding
Of the fear
Glad to let the trauma go.

Letting go

I set off early one morning
With 2 young women
Healer friends
We travelled through the glorious
Verdant English countryside
On a beautiful summer day
To visit Avebury
An ancient stone circle
Of power and magic.

On arrival we sensed our personal stones
Sat by them
Soaking up their vibrations
Recharging ourselves

Drawn to the centre
Of a small inner circle
An area of
Soft, gentle energy
We sat
Exchanged healing

One cherished
The sister receiving
Channelled healing to her
One sat at her feet to sooth
Allowing the healing to flow
Throughout her entire body.

We took turns
Cherishing
Receiving
Soothing

Ana

She came
Fresh
Eager
Keen to learn
The mystery
Of crystals

We talked about
Auras and chakras
Experienced the energy
Of various crystals
Their empathy
With the human body

After several sessions
Ana started to talk about
Her love of
Sacred geometry
Her affiliation with
Tectonic plates

We went off piste
Changed the direction
Of learning
Explored
Earth healing
Regression
Past life memories

Ana unfolded
Integrated her new knowledge
Began to glow

I took her back in time
To her origin
Her soul star
She felt empowered

I was on new ground too
Totally abandoned
My curriculum
Worked completely intuitively
Each time she came
Both of us learning

Ana started working with
Tectonic energies
Sacred shapes
Tuning into higher planes
Welcomed Dragons into her life
All new knowledge

'I don't know where I'm going'
I confessed
'You are the only one
Who takes me to
These new awarenesses'
She replied
' Please continue'

Together we unfolded
Me by leading her
Wherever my intuition guided
She discovering more
About her gifts
How to use them
Growing in confidence

Ana still returns for more
I take a breath
Tune in
Trust
We dive deeper
Fly higher
Discover more truths
Together

Soul journeying

My soul went into deep deep mourning
At the parting of a young friend
For several days
My body recoiled
Curled up
I withdrew into a strange place
Between realms
Unable to move

My soul was journeying
Accompanying the soul of this dear young man
Guiding him on to new pastures
After his time had come
To leave this Earth

His soul travelled on
Towards the light
Guided to its new home

He is safe.

Preparation for birth.

I was working at the healing clinic where I volunteer when a very pregnant lady came through the door and asked if I could give her healing.

She explained she was feeling very uncomfortable, heavy and anxious about giving birth.

As she lay on the couch I guided her into a deep relaxation surrounding her with pale pink light. Whilst I was giving the healing I had the vision that I was working down her spine as if I was preparing her body for birth.

I communed with the baby's soul saying it was safe to be born when it felt ready. I also communed with the mother's soul reassuring her it was safe to let go and give birth when she felt ready.

After the 30 minute healing the mother-to-be felt much lighter and very relaxed. When she stood up she seemed much taller.

We chatted about her going home and surrounding herself with pale pink colours and rose essence for nurture and allowing herself to rest in preparation for birth.

I heard from the mother a few days later that she had gone home and covered her bed in pale pink blankets, sprinkled rose essence in her room and slept. That evening she went into labour and after a quick, easy birth was blessed with a healthy little girl. The mother was most grateful for the healing preparation and delighted to have easy home birth assisted by a midwife.

What a wonderful experience to be part of. I felt honoured to have offered such comfort and insight.

****

In ancient Egypt the wise women healers and midwives used colours and crystals to assist in birth. They had birthing pools of coloured water to support and comfort the mother during delivery. Around the birthing pools crystals would be placed and the mother guided to choose the crystal which would assist with the birthing process.

I have had past life visions of offering colour and crystal birth therapy in Ancient Egypt and am pleased that my soul could tap into this ancient wisdom.

Working with fertility.

A young woman heard a female friend talking about her healing experience with me, extoling my gifts as a healer. The young woman rang me and booked for a healing session. She arrived wearing a black tightly buttoned coat.
She confided she had tried IVF treatment and felt her body had gone into shock. She was feeling pressured to continue but no longer wished to follow through with the IVF.
After guiding her into deeper relaxation and surrounding her with pink light I held my hands over her ovaries and asked her what she could sense and 'see'.
My client said her ovaries were surrounded by darkness. I guided her to breath the light into them and start to talk to her ovaries asking them what they needed.
Her ovaries 'replied' they were in hiding after the IVF.
This young woman was very sensitive and receptive to the healing therapy, able to speak to her body and find answers. After several sessions of crystal healing she ran up my path wearing colourful, very feminine flowered clothes.
What a noticeable change in her and her appearance. She felt delighted to feel in touch with her femininity once again. During one session she communed with her ovaries and asked them if they were ready to try again with the fertility treatment.
We talked about supporting herself and her ovaries through the IVF process with meditation, yoga, healing and rest.
This time the treatment was successful.
We worked together throughout the pregnancy with individual 1-1 sessions and supportive phone calls.
The happy ending of this story was the birth of a beautiful daughter.

My young client was besotted with her baby and thoroughly enjoying every aspect of motherhood.
It was such a precious process to guide a young woman to reconnect with her femininity and her deep yearning for motherhood.
*****

I have had several young high flying career women who feel out of touch with their femininity.
Through the healing process I see them embrace change, soften, nurture themselves and bring their feminine qualities into their prestigious jobs.
You can be soft strong intelligent and in touch with your femininity!!

Close Encounters with the Medical Profession
and
Aiding healing with visualisation and crystals.

The day had arrived. With mild trepidation I had set off for the local hospital for a simple, minor operation to remove a small cyst from the front of my scalp.

I was approached by a nurse looking for patients and was whisked away to a changing cubicle where I was instructed to change into an operating gown.

'Change into a gown for a minor head operation?' I asked. I'd expected to sit in a chair for this simple procedure, fully clothed. I certainly hadn't anticipated changing and had not prepared myself by donning my best underwear. 'Do I really need a gown ?'

' You can keep your trousers on I suppose' came the concession from the nurse.

I asked the nurse if she would tie the tapes at the back of the mausoleum gown I had been given to wear, as they were difficult to reach.

'Oh you don't need to bother about that, put your clothes in that red plastic basket and follow me' she replied.

'Anyway, the gown is probably more comfortable undone'

The gown may have been physically more comfortable undone, but for me it was psychologically very uncomfortable.

'Phase one of the dehumanizing process' I thought, as I walked through the corridors wearing a hospital gown gaping open at the back and carrying a red plastic basket with my clothes in. Thank goodness I had at least been allowed to keep my trousers on.

I followed the nurse to the operating theatre and was left alone, sitting in a corner on a plastic chair with my plastic basket waiting for the doctor. I felt like a bag woman.

After a wait of about 15 minutes, a young female doctor bounced into the operating theatre. After signing an operating form handed to me the doctor announced in a very loud voice
'I'll start by shaving her head at the front.'
There was no Hello, no How are you? No introduction, no handshake- in fact no human interaction or recognition of me at all- not the way I greet my clients.
I summoned up the courage to say
'Is it really necessary to shave my hair off as my hair is really fine and I'm sure it will flatten down.'

'I'll do as little as I can' the doctor replied, pulling really hard at my hair.
I caught the eye of a nurse who seemed to understand my concern. She winked at me and quickly chipped in
'I'll do that with my scissors. Doctor'
The kind nurse cut not a single hair but managed to part and flatten it with antiseptic lotion leaving an exposed patch of scalp around the cyst.
Bravo - someone with a human touch.
I was invited to get up onto the operating couch and make myself comfortable lying down. I looked around for a step or stool to help me climb up, but found nothing of the kind. I hauled myself up onto the couch in a rather ungainly manner.
Did this really have to be so difficult and undignified I wondered?
A few moments passed as I lay on the couch with my eyes shut.
I was preparing myself for the operation with meditation, visualizing white light flowing through my body.
Somebody walked up to me and asked
'Are you comfortable there?'

'Yes thank you' I replied, touched at the caring enquiry.
'Well you soon won't be 'came the fast quip.
My heart sank. Such tender care- well what had I expected? This lack of loving care became more intense. I tried to return to my meditative state and concentrate on inner peace and light.
The doctor stood at the head of the couch, ready to start the operation.
'Have you given the anaesthetic ?' She asked the operating nurses.
'No doctor, that is your job at this hospital' one of the nurses replied.
'O.K. What anaesthetic do you usually use here? I know, let's use one with adrenalin in it. Do you think 50mls will be enough ?' asked the doctor.
Oh God, I thought, do I really need adrenalin pumping around my body and why don't you know before the operation which anaesthetic to use and how much to give?
'Don't panic ' I said to reassure myself. 'Just relax and focus on channelling light'

'Are you still with us?' asked the doctor.
'Yes' I assured her.
'Well this is going to hurt, this is the worst bit. I'm just injecting the anaesthetic into your scalp'
To my amazement, I only felt a tiny prick-'The light is working' I thought.
'This is going to hurt again' came the doctor's voice.
'I'd prefer it if you don't tell me what you're doing. I won't feel anything if I just meditate through this, you see I'm a healer.'
'Well you're not much of an advert for healing if you've had to come here, are you ?' was the doctor's response.

'Well if you remove the physical lump, the healing will do the rest.' I said 'I would like to keep meditating through this and lie quietly, please.'

'That's unusual. Most people want to know exactly what I'm doing.' said the doctor.

Oh God. Please help me! What had happened to tender loving care, soft words and kindness? I went back to my meditation and concentrated on focusing light to my head.

'These pillow cases are an unusual colour,' came the doctor's voice.

A conversation ensued between the doctor and the nurses about the hospital linen !!!

Do I laugh or shout angrily, 'Hello what about me here- your patient on the couch?'

Maybe it was the effect of the adrenalin, but I did feel like hitting someone.

'Pass the instruments please.' the doctor again.

I heard, rather than felt, a cut on my scalp and rough hard hands pushing my head.

'Oh, are the instruments sterile, nurse?'

It's a bit late to ask after you've made the incision!

'There we are, cyst removed. I'll just stitch up the cut-are you still with us down there?'

'Yes thank you I'm O.K.'

I felt the needle forcing its way through my scalp.

'These suture needles aren't much good- they aren't fine enough for this kind of work.' said the doctor.

What confidence these people inspire!

'Well at least the suture material is blue and will show up in her grey hair nicely. I'll leave really long ends. You know, it would be so much easier if they just completely shaved the heads of all these patients.'

Someone came to stand next to me and touched my shoulder.

'Can you hear me?' she said.
'Yes, thank you.' I replied.
At last some tender loving care, a kind voice and a gentle holding of my hand to help me relax.
'When you get home the pain will really kick in. Take 2 paracetamol every 4 hours. Do you understand about the pain? Can you hear me? Go to your G.P. in 2 week's time and have the stitches removed. If the pain gets too much, keep taking the paracetamol.'
Oh yes, I can hear you and I'm trying really hard not to. Why are people so keen to tell me about pain? Whatever happened to TLC?
'All finished now. You can get up and go.'
'Would it be alright if I just lie here for a few moments, please?' I asked
'I would like a few moments to do some self-healing.'
I lay still and returned to the light focusing exercise.
I visualized sewing up the incision area, taking away all pain and repairing the hole in my aura. I was granted one minute's peace then a voice said
'Come and sit over here please.'
I got up and went to sit on a plastic chair at the side of the room.
'Put this on your head and hold it on tight.'
The operating theatre had emptied, just me and a nurse remained.
'Right, don't wet your hair for a week dear.'
I caught sight of myself in a mirror- oh no! Red antiseptic all over my head and I wasn't supposed to wash it for a week! It looked great with the long blue stitches. My face and neck were scarlet- the effect of the adrenalin I presumed- what a sight I looked. I tried to rearrange my locks before walking outside- it had never occurred to me to bring a hat.

Back home, feeling rather fragile and battered, I made up my mind I would not need paracetamol. I began my own care programme. First I drank lots of cold water to wash the adrenalin out of my system. Then I lay down and psychically projected light for 15 minutes through a single terminated quartz crystal pointed at the incision area to repair all damage and remove all pain. I did not feel any pain at all and the wound healed beautifully, much to the surprise of the doctor.

****

I would like to acknowledge the power of the visualising light in aiding healing and the use of a single terminated crystal to direct light to the chosen site of healing. This knowledge can really compliment medical practises.

I would also like to send a plea to doctors to treat patients with kindness and humanity from the moment they arrive till the moment they depart. I know kindness and gentleness help healing, they certainly make the patient feel calm and at ease.

VISIONS
and
DREAMS

I have visions of
Times gone by
Access to ancient wisdoms
Karmic patterns

Chakra Flow

It was the end
Of a busy day
Teaching
Thirty little children
In my class

My head was pounding
I was ready to go home
When a young girl
Came up to me
To ask a question
I bent down to answer her
Giving her a warm smile
And my time

Finally I arrived home
Head still pounding
I leaned backwards
Over the arm of a chair

Suddenly
Colours started to flow
Through me
From the base of my spine
To the crown of my head
All the colours of the rainbow
Red
Orange
Yellow
Green
Blue
Violet
Magenta

Chakra aligned
A rainbow of colours flowed
Continuously through me

My head cleared
I felt wonderful
Uplifted
Serene
Energised
Calm

For 5 weeks following
This experience
I had no need of
Sleep or Food
Energy just flowed
I must have glowed
Many people were drawn to me
Constantly seeking my company
My wisdom
I was in total balance
Chakras aligned
A magical state
Of connection
Oneness

Although a little overwhelmed
To experience such a glow
I have often tried
To recreate this state of being
I get close when I do energy channelling
Especially of Angels
The full moon
and
Goddesses.

Reforming chemical bonds

As a young student of biochemistry
I could 'see' chemical reactions
Taking place in the test tube.
I was unaware that this was
A special gift

In the test tube
Bond broke
Reformed
Recreated
Electrons flying
Chemicals transforming
Poetry in motion
Chemical reaction

The Coachman

My new home is really old
Built in 1885 as the coach house
To the manor house next door
As we settled in
I saw him standing
Between the old coach shed and
The house
The Coachman
Dressed in ancient caped-cloak
A brown, shadowy figure
Observing
He appeared several times
During the first six months
Silent, watchful,
Guardian of his former home.
I no longer see him and feel sure
He must approve of our presence
Continuing life in
His old coach-house

The Gold shoes

My son's graduation!!
How fine
I found a gold Indian silk outfit-
Not my usual style
But-hey I can be a proud mother in this!!
Hmmm- shoes
My tatty old dance shoes do not look good
With this outfit
In Saffron Walden to meet my daughter
Just popped in Lily's to check out shoes!!
Suddenly
I entered a time zone,
A light space,
Another dimension
Of golden light
I turned
And there they were
Shining on a stand
Like a trophy
On it's pedestal
The GOLD SHOES.
I tried them on
Just perfect
So I bought the gold shoes
Guided from the other side
By my mum

OPENING - a vision

My essence was
Encased in a
Pale blue coating
Of
Sweetness
Peacefulness.

This coating is cracking open
To reveal a core
Of very dark chocolate
Chocolate full of
Richness
Nurture
Vitality
Connection
Ancient knowledge
Strength
Magical healing properties

The chocolate is
M
E
L
T
I
N
G
Flowing
Thick and free
Pouring an elixir of
Hope
Courage
Freedom

Throughout my being
Allowing my soul gifts
To be fully presenced
Into the world.

New Purple Wings

I was given
New wings!
They are made of
Long, deep purple feathers
To use for
Protection, strength.

BUT
They felt
Heavy
Clumsy
Unwieldy

I was excited to
Have new wings
although
They felt like a
Burden

I rested for several days
Stretched and flexed
my wings
Now they are
HUGE
FLUFFY
Angels wing
Mauve topped
Graduating to
Deep purple
Tips.

They are for
Maturity
Strength
Protection

I am beginning
to enjoy
These new wings
Which I have
Earned.

Pink Tara's Gift

Lost
Looking for a place to spend the night
I came across a tiny Buddhist temple
Isolated on the Coromandel Peninsular
In new Zealand
I asked if I could stay
The night
There was one room available
For guests

I joined the morning meditation
Sat cross-legged on my cushion
Drifted away with the mantras
Goddess Pink Tara
Appeared before me
Held out her hand
Placed a pink lotus on my lips
Ensuring I would always speak with
Softness
Kindness
Love
Acceptance

I thanked
The Goddess Pink Tara
For my beautiful gift
I felt very blessed.

Lady's smock

As a young child
About 8 years old
I remember a day
Out wildflower spotting
With my mother and 2 sisters
My mum
Pointed out a
Lady's smock
Over a fence
In the middle of a marshy area

For a moment
I tapped into
A super-power
Rose out of my body
Moved towards the flower
Where the marsh forbade us walk
Took a close look
At the tiny mauvy pink petals
Admired their beauty
Delicacy
This became a
Favourite flower of mine
And
A magical moment
I have always
Treasured.

Transformation with Archangels

Deep diving into the dark mud
with Archangel Tzaphkiel
Releasing old patterns
Cleansing on many levels

Swirling in the whirlwind
Of Archangel Zuriel
Drawn into a new dimension
Of pale pink light

I feel soft, gentle
Fine, Ethereal
Light, delicate.

I have entered a new way of being
All knowing
All seeing
Wise

Sister Moon

She called
I answered
'Share my love
Energy, wisdom'
she said
'I will ' I replied
'Whenever you call
I am happy to be
of service'

OH what beauty
She shared
Messages of
LOVE
BEAUTY
WISDOM
HOPE
COURAGE
FORTITUDE
JUSTICE
HEALING
PEACE

I felt humbled,
Honoured
To be her partner
Spreading such
Wonderous gifts
Across our world
Waking up and welcoming
Souls to
DIVINE FEMININE
POWER

<u>So spoke the Ash</u>

I placed my hand
against a tall Ash tree
Which stood sentinel in
a magical Ash ring

'Stand tall and elegant like me'
she said
'Live from your core being,
Be strong,
Spread your arms wide
like my branches
to welcome others

Let go of the past
for there is no past
only NOW
the present.
Live with Love
All will be well'

Thank you dear Ash
Bless you for your
Wisdom

EARTH HEALING
GRIDS
And
PORTALS

I set light grids
Across the planet
Open portals
Create golden webs
Connecting sacred sites
To cleanse
Heal
Rebalance

Setting Energy Grids around the World

I've often felt called to different parts of the world. When visiting I've had that extraordinary Honour and Grace to be chosen to set energetic grids and raise the vibration of the place I'm visiting.
I'm sharing a few of my experiences.

Lucca, Italy

I was cycling around the ancient city walls of Lucca in Tuscany with some of my friends. As I was flying along, enjoying the wind in my hair and the views of the amazing architecture of this ancient city I felt my vibrations raise, opening my third eye and Crown. I put down my feet, pause my cycling and focused on what was being asked of me.
A beautiful sparkling golden web streamed forth from my third eye right across the entirety of this ancient city. The purpose of this web was to raise the vibration of Lucca, bringing light back to this city, whose name means LIGHT.

Maui, Hawaii

I rather rashly booked on the writers course in Maui, Hawaii. I booked a very inexpensive room, found a newly opened economy flight which suited my limited budget and off I went.
I arrived at my accommodation in the evening and it was already dark. To my consternation I was dropped at a small old building about 4 minutes from the main hotel and I had to clamber up three flights of steps on an old metal fire escape to my room.
I was shown in to a spacious but very dated bedroom with an extremely basic bathroom.
I went to bed and tried to sleep wondering what I'd done booking such an inexpensive room.

On waking I thought I could hear water. I open the curtains and to my extreme delight my room was on the beach and the balcony overlooked palm trees and golden sand. Beautiful!! 'How amazing' I thought and smiled. Of course I got exactly the right room, how could I have even doubted-I'm always guided !?

My accommodation was perfect for me. Quiet, secluded, on the beach with beautiful views and beautiful sunsets.

One evening as I sat on my balcony I felt my energy rise. I was guided to set a beautiful grid of bright white light all the way around the island. The grid was to purify the water and reactivate the light of Maui.

What a gift and honour to be able to assist in this magical process.

Of course I was 'taken' there and was well looked after!!!

The River Thames, London

I was invited to attend a Mind Body and Spirit festival in London with young friends I'd recently met. It was many years since I participated in one of these festivals and kept wondering why I was there.

After visiting the festival we hailed a taxi to take us to meet some other friends of my young companions.

As we were on a bridge driving over the River Thames a beautiful white bridge issued forth from my third eye all along the Thames in both directions for greater purification of the water.

'Ah' I said 'now I know why I'm here!'

I shared my experience of setting the grid. My young friends clapped and cheered said 'Well done!!!'

These are just a few of the many, many grids I have set round the globe to raise the vibrations bringing the planet to alignment with the DIVNE FEMININE energies returning to the Earth at this present time.

A Thousand Petalled Lotus

Sitting on my sofa
Preparing myself
To host a workshop on
Attuning to the Divine feminine
I went into a place
Of deep reverie
Connected
Tuned in
'elsewhere'

I saw
A THOUSAND PETALLED LOTUS
Spread across the floor
Of the room where I would be working
And white, opalescent, glowing Lotus
In full bloom
With a
Golden centre
Set as a grid of
Divine feminine beauty

I felt blessed
To have created
This glorious energy
In which to
BE

A Visit to Stonehenge

As I approached the circle of stones
Standing sentinel
In the open landscape
I perceived a small group of men
Clothed in long rustic capes
From eons gone by
Gathered around the edge
Of the inner circle-
A meeting of the higher council.

On the central stone
A Goddess stood majestically
Long light robe shimmering
Flowing in the gentle breeze
A metallic crescent-moon crown
Adorning her head
Enabling her to channel higher wisdom
Become an oracle

As I stood watching
A golden spiral slowly rose
From beneath the temple
Forming a golden circle around the site
A great flame-coloured burst of energy
Appeared within the centre of the stones
Reigniting this ancient portal.

Golden lines radiated outwards
Forming a network
Connecting many many ancient sites
Castlerigg, Arbour Low
The Merry Maidens, Avebury
To name but a few
Renewing connections
Resetting energetic grids

My work here is done.

The Merry Maidens
Standing stones in Cornwall

All day long
I felt overwhelmed by
Waves of deep sorrow
Releasing through my heart
I just wanted to cry and cry
A never-ending stream
of tears
For no apparent reason

Later in the day
I felt called to visit
An ancient circle of
Standing stones
Over 4,000 years old
Named
The Merry Maidens

As I stepped through the gate
Into the field hosting the stones
It felt as though
I'd stepped through a portal
Into soft eternal
Sacred space

I walked towards the stones
Drawn to one particular maiden
Once again I felt overwhelmed
By deep
Deep sorrow

I leaned against my chosen maiden
Allowed sorrow to
Rise within me
Wondering why the Merry Maidens
were so so sad

I asked the universe
'What is my role here?'
In my vision a multi-pointed
golden star-shaped grid
Began to form
Linking the maidens
Glowing and growing in
Intensity

I wandered around the circle
Blessing each maiden
With a tender touch
And loving heart
Entered the sacred centre
Where the sun beamed down upon me
Creating a portal of golden light
Linking heaven and earth

This portal is set
As one of many
Across the world
To remove all female sadness
From our earth
Dating back eons
The stones began to lighten
Stand proud
Shine
The Maidens
Felt Merry once more!

I sat a little longer
With this vision
Helping the golden grid
Grow stronger
The sunlight portal
Strengthen
Eventually
The Merry Maidens smiled
Happy once more
My work here was done
I felt blessed

Arbor Low

I walked through a veil of
Softness, tranquillity, peace
Approaching the ancient site of
Arbor Low
A stone circle 6,000 years old
High upon the Derbyshire peaks.
The circle is surrounded by a mound
Hiding the stones within
Stones flattened by those who
Feared their power

I was drawn towards 'my' stone
Where I sat and tuned in
I sensed alternate stones hold
Male or female energy
'My ' stone was of male energy
Strong vibrations
Tingled through my hands

In my mind's eye
A golden circle appeared above the ring
Joined to each stone by a
Fine golden thread
In the centre of the circle
Appeared a golden flame
Opening a portal
Connecting to the ancient
God of Thunder
The sky
The elements
This was the site of
Initiation into the brotherhood of
Thor

As I entered the centre I felt lifted
A golden grid connected beneath the stones
The central golden flame
Took on a complex geometric design.
This was a re-awakening
Of a power portal
Connection
To the sky
The elements
Invoking
Physical strength
Protection

Connecting the Rings

We found it-
Isolated in North Cumbria UK
Castlerigg Stone Circle
Majestic standing stones
On ancient hill top.

My daughter laughed as I walked round
For I was dressed in pink sparkly top
Pink sparkly flipflops
Diaphanous silk scarf
Whilst fellow visitors
Sported heavy walking boots,
Anoraks, hats and gloves.

Smiling to myself
I wandered round
Drawn to one particular stone
Which I stood by
And lovingly caressed.

Suddenly in my mind's eye
I 'saw' rings of golden light
Spinning round the circle of stones
Grounding with a flash
Through the centre
Of the circle
Connecting the energy
With the standing stones in
Avebury.

Ah I thought
So that is why I am here-
To connect these ancient stone circles
Reactivating their sacred energy.

*

(I really didn't need walking boots for that!)

Nine Ladies

Walking along the path
Through wooded glade
Light drizzle
Refreshing the way

Birds singing
Cuckoo calling
'Keep going
Keep going'
Guiding the way

My eyes were drawn
To a soft velvety Dell
Moist grass glistened
Creating a silvery carpet
On which stood
The Nine Ladies
An ancient stone circle

I walked the circle
Entered the delicate atmosphere
Lightly touched every stone
Paying homage to each

An underground connection formed
To Castlerigg Stones
Linking the circles
Energy surged into
The Nine Ladies ring

Slowly the sleeping Ladies
Awakened from a long slumber
Started to uncurl
Stretch
Regain their freedom
Restoring the Divine Feminine
Gifts of
Softness
Gentleness
Delicacy
Nurture
Discretion
Magic
To the stones

Visiting Glastonbury and Avebury

I journeyed to Glastonbury
With my spiritual teacher
And a friend
We walked the female labyrinth path
Up to the Tor
Drank from the Chalice well
Climbed Wearyall Hill
To see the Holy Thorn.

Travelling home
My car veered off the road
Following a sign
To Avebury
My favourite magical site
Of ancient standing stones.

We arrived at Twilight
Stones lit by a full moon
Set off for a short walk
In a mystical atmosphere

My spiritual teacher
Danced a funny little dance
We laughed
Waved our arms
Honoured the stones
Returned home.
**

The following day
A psychic friend
Knocked on my teacher's door
Declared
'You opened a portal
From Avebury to your healing room'

In our next meditation circle
I felt the dark pull
Of many lost souls
Calling for help
'We are not a rescue circle my dear'
Said my teacher
But I could not remain silent
I was overwhelmed
Dragged down by the sorrow
And fear of so many souls calling

'We have to help' I insisted
We all sent light
To the centre of the circle
I saw a ladder
Ascend from a deep dark place
Hundreds and hundreds of lost souls
Men women children
Climbed up the rungs
Led by one brave soul
Carrying a dim lantern
Guided towards the light
Through the portal we had created
At Avebury

'Thank you thank you thank you so much '
They cried
Their fear abated
Their souls raised up
Released to the light

I felt a huge relief
Lightness return
I had played my part
Guiding many lost souls
Back to the light.

Labyrinth walk

On beginning my sacred walk
Around an ancient
Labyrinth
I asked the question
'How can I move forward?'
The answer came
' Share your knowledge
Widen your horizons
Touch more people
And enjoy being
YOU
Write talk
Run workshops
Go where you are called
Set healing grids
Where needed
Open portals of light
Commune with the Moon Goddesses
Angels
Ascended Masters
Giving messages of solace
Comfort
Growth
Have fun doing this
Be free to be yourself
Sharing your gifts.'

After this sacred walk
I stood looking over
At the labyrinth
A golden grid started to shine
Across the maze
A multitude of fairies
Danced all around
Happy the golden energy
was restored
And reconnected.

As my friend
Stood in the centre
Of the maze
She felt a very strong
Energy
Grounding through her
Reopening the Dragon portal
Of the Labyrinth.

A job well done
The Fairies and Dragons
Are happy
Once again.

Ely Cathedral

Sitting on a bench
Overlooking the grand
Old Cathedral
In Ely
Bathed in a golden evening glow
I closed my eyes
Asked for guidance
'Oh my goodness
How heavy this place is'
My soul cried!
'How can I help?'

I saw a vision of
A huge bright heart
Filling the interior of this
Grand Cathedral
Spinning white light
Lifting
Renewing
Cleansing.

I heard the message
'To bring this place
Into alignment
with the new
It needs to invite people in.
Open its doors to all
Welcome
Music
Art
Drama
Dance
Song
Poetry

Begone with the old fusty ways
Of just reading the Bible
Rekindle
Reconnect
BRING IN LIFE
Offer
HOPE
LOVE
CHARITY
Support people to find
Self-worth
Recover from pain
Walk a new path of
Creativity
Cooperation
Fulfilment
Oneness.
Teach
LOVE
By example'

<u>Golden Caribbean Grid</u>

Floating on my back
In warm, crystal clear
Buoyant sea water
Under a brilliant blue sky
On a deserted Caribbean beach
Quiet
Solitary
At peace
I was guided to draw down
The sunlight to form
A golden geometric grid
All around the island
Raising its vibration
Lifting a cloud of
Dark karma
Of eons gone by
Restoring lightness
Life
Breath
To the beautiful
Island of
Tobago.

Puerto Vallarta Mexico
1

I'd been having
Visions
Of golden lines
Crossing the earth and oceans
Focusing on one sacred point of
POWER
Close to Puerto Vallarta

The lines gathered in intensity
Glittering
Activating
Converging
As we neared the
NEW MOON
In preparation for setting
An energetic grid
Opening a new portal
Connecting to the cosmos
To bring
Healing
Restore harmony
Bring light
Rebalance our planet.

Opening a Portal at Puerto Vallarta 2

Three of us sat
On the roof terrace of
Casa De Influencia

I tuned in
Saw a great explosion
Of bright white light
At the convergence of the
Many ley lines
Just off Los Arcos

The bright white light
Washed over us
Cleansing our personal space
Entered the crown of
Our heads
Flowed down to our hearts
We connected
Heart to heart
Forming a scared triangle
Of stability
Dedication
To helping each other
Fulfil our
Soul purpose
**

Above our heads
A point of light connected to
Our hearts
Creating a triangular
Pyramid of trust
Light flowed from our hearts
Down to the soles of our feet
Connected us to
The core of the earth

From the core
A soft orange light
Of
JOY
Flowed up to our hearts
Creating a pyramid
Of orange light
***
A sacred triangular bi-prism
Was formed
Bringing bright portal light
And orange
Earth energy
To
Casa De Influencia
Through our hearts.
Dedicating this house
To helping others
On their spiritual path
***

Such beauty.
***

The three of us
In a past life had been part of an intergalactic council
We'd been brought back together to open this portal and set
a sacred grid.

LYON

Just after the riots
I 'saw'
A bright light
Shining over
La Basilique Notre Dame
Lifting a dark cloud

A fine mesh of
White light
Flowed along the
Rivers Rhône and Saône
Cleansing and purifying
Their waters

Peace was restored.

FINALE

GIFTS

Empathy
Sensitivity
Connection
Mysticism
Are wonderful gifts to bring to the world
BUT
To those who have them
It can be a challenge to navigate
An 'ordinary' life
SO
Please be kind to us
Treat us with reverence
Heed our words
For we are here
To bring
Love
Understanding
Healing
Peace
Enlightenment
Harmony
Justice
Equality
and
Magic
x

About The Author

Suzanna Magic is a Teacher, Healer, Mystic.
Suzanna is mother to 3 wonderful children and grandmother to 7 precious grandchildren.
As a child she was very sensitive and felt as though she did not really belong here.
Suzanna had many 'weird' experiences which she now understands to be spiritual experiences.
Suzanna was quiet but knew she was wise!! Now she understands she is an empath.
Suzanna graduated with a BSc. honours degree in Biochemistry and felt a calling to teach.
Suzanna has taught across all age ranges.
Suzanna followed an interest in complementary therapies qualifying as a Healer, Colour Therapist, Crystal Therapist, Counsellor, Play Therapist and Child Advocate.
Suzanna hosts psychic development circles, teaches colour and crystal therapy and sees clients 1-1.
Suzanna hosts Full moon meditations online where she channels Goddess energies and wisdom, crystal and colour energies to help bring Divine Feminine energy to earth.
To follow a Full Moon meditation click FB link below.
Suzanna is an Earth Healer and is called to sacred sites to set energy grids which re-activate power points across the planet.
Suzanna feels her soul-purpose is to foster an understanding of spirituality, nurture others on their soul journey and bring Divine Feminine energy to earth.
Suzanna writes poetry and short stories about her spiritual experiences.
****

Suzanna's qualifications - B.Sc. Hons. Cert. Ed., Member
Healing Trust, Dip. Colour Therapy,
Dip. Crystal Therapy, P.C. Counselling, Cert. Play Therapy,
Child Advocacy diploma
****

Connect with Suzanna
www.suzannahealer.co.uk
colourfulsuz@gmail.com
fb.me/suzannasunflowersanctuary
****

<u>Suzanna Magic's choice of font and colours</u>

<u>Font</u>
I chose comic sans as the font for my book of poems as it is my understanding that it is the easiest
for the human eye to read. It is certainly easiest on my eyes.
The British Dyslexia Association recommends Comic Sans, noting that
"letters can appear less crowded" than with other fonts.

<u>My understanding of Colours</u>
Purple- wisdom, maturity, depth
Magenta- self-love, self-awareness and self-acceptance
Blue- healing, inner-peace
Turquoise- visions, dreams, etheric realms
Gold- energy, light, power

Each colour has its own vibrational frequency which adds another dimension to my words.
Enjoy !!!

Reader Love

Dear Suzanna
Feminine Soul sister
Light worker
A feminine warrior
Beautiful poems
I salute your clarity of purpose
I resonate with so much of what you shared
of the why you are here on this planet now.
I salute and admire your divine Feminine power,
your presence and the grace and courage in which you handle
Your callings on all arenas
With love and admiration
x

I am so excited to see the opening poem in your book and how your poem links the chapters together. I love how you are presencing yourself boldly and powerfully. Congratulations.
x

Thank you for your poems. They are beautiful and SO ARE YOU.
All these amazing gifts you have fill me with awe and I'm also aware of the responsibility that comes with them.
Thinking of you my dear friend in your duties as protector and healer of the world.
Lots of love
x

Your poems captured and embraced your beauty as a person, spiritual being and beyond.
x

Thank you for your groups and the compassionate nurturing that fill them before, during and after each session. Your careful kindness is rich indeed. With much love
x

How I LOVE reading your poems .
I want to shout it from the mountaintops-
"Yes Mrs. Magic is such a gift to all who know her, to the world and the universe as she travels in all kinds of dimensions to the places that need the healing that she so generously and lovingly gifts though it can be exhausting and painful at times."
It is a soulful and magical joy to know you and love you and witness as well as hear of your amazing miracles and to bask in your love and spirit and genius!
Wishing you all the best always and sending you so much love
x

As I read your poems I am in Awe of this power and gift you so gracefully own. Three cheers for your courage, boldness, and your innate desire to serve the world through your spiritual gifts.
Very Bold and Beautiful, Mrs. Magic
x

Your poetry is wonderful- you capture and express the energy of the divine in just a few words. Your constant willingness to support others with your gifts is remarkable.
Your willingness to help, your will to serve life and people.
Your trust in your tangible connection to the divine.
Your words in your poems are like magic pearls.
x

At the centre and root of my achievements there is always your constant companionship, love, light, magic, healing and non-judgemental support.
I love you and know our beautiful, timeless connection and blessed friendship will continue to evolve with love, hope, joy, faith, peace and boundless beauty at the centre.
Sending lots and lots of love & light.
x

The value you bring to the healing process is spot on and I really love that you can connect with younger women. They are yearning for sage role models and female mentors, which I so easily see in you.
Thank you so much Suzanna- you have a gift!
x

Suzanna you are such a treasure....You often don't realise how much your light and love and your generosity of spirit balance and quell the un-tempered souls around us.
It's unspoken, often unseen but it is definitely felt. It's an energetic hug to those who dwell in the lower realms.
As you say... Love heals All
x

Suzanna exudes a uniquely beautiful energy which amplifies any workshop,
meditation or teaching experience she is facilitating.
I have had the pleasure of all three and been awed and delighted in equal measure.
x

Suzanna, I see a wise, powerful healer and messenger in you!
x

Suzanna you're a very inspirational woman, possessed of many gifts and talents and I always feel I shine more brightly in your presence.
That in itself is a treasure and I thank you for it.
x

Thank you so much for being there as a beacon of light for all of us who need some guidance on our soul paths.
Your magic works wonders and makes a difference in this world.
x